momentary

Hiru Batepola

BookLeaf Publishing

India | USA | UK

Presentation by *BookLeaf Publishing*

Web: www.bookleafpub.com

E-mail: info@bookleafpub.com

ISBN: 9789357447089

First edition 2021

fossils in my manuscript

my pages are not yellow from neglect
they age like amber
immortal
my skeleton trapped in verse

-

she waits patiently
for my visit
and when I arrive
under starry skies my skeleton and I
run hand in hand until dawn

aurora borealis

sleep on Polaris light
let the fuzzy Rapture whirl;
the dizzy curl of colour, sweep away
that cold insomnia
creeping into dawn
deep in starry arms until
the Spectacle fades

I love the way you make my bed

how you pull my duvet
over our shadows
how you brush the whispers off
my pillows -
little peonies fly in the wind,
at the touch of your hand.
they were left too long in the sun,
dry and wasting in the late afternoon.
it was the strangest thing -
not long after you left,
I shook the duvet of old spice,
and a thousand little clocks spilled out!
they still sit on the floor, ticking away...

summer song

hazy sun
drips into the ocean
teenagers slink
behind the sunset on
Lover's Rock
soft skin soaked
in salt and lime
they lament at
the Spanish flute
who sings so predictably
to the drunken tourists,
"tú eres todo para mí"

insecurity

I act like I don't care
like it's nothing I haven't heard before
but I still collect your compliments like
loose change
gold coins
for a vending machine on a rainy day
I still collect your promises like
keychains in a tourist shop
For when I fly away
Or you do

Sometimes it's not awful

sometimes it's not awful
to watch the sun dip into the lake in the
evening
and witness the drunken flies
making their rounds

it's not so awful
to feel the breeze from the river
or the gin at the back of my throat

suppose it wasn't terrible
to gaze at the sweaters in the sand
and wonder how they got there
if they belonged to two lovers
who last evening kissed each other
goodbye
for the last time
and find now

it's not as awful as they thought
without each other

prelude to autumn

Late August
is a hare
leaping through cornfields
it twangs like a folk singer
who strums madly on brazen strings
in a final crescendo

autumn song

dried leaves rest on windswept weeds,
among walnuts,
and oak trees,
dead butterflies on the autumn breeze.
glimmering breath of spring,
mossy tensions of the summer stream,
all cool down for frozen, forgotten -
wasted! winter dreams.

support system

cup my face in your
hands, drink my words as they drool
puddles in your palms
lick my laughter and wipe off
my nonsensical
sorrow, my aimless mutter

fear of failure

the dreamers never leave me
their mist around my ankles
the careless Myth of tomorrow be
haunts my easy tranquil

my affectionate

my affectionate -
cast your eyes
unto my reflection,
ripples in space -
echoes across the universe,
our love encapsulate
waves holding glass bottles
roll into Atlantis
all the sea folk -
gaze up to the surface
"it's happened again,"
the dolphins exclaim,
"a love as boundless as the ocean!"

The Magpie

the Magpie hovers
over the dreary, sick,
diseased October;
infested with grey, she is
looking for cobwebs
of gems, thrifty bird.

winter in the city

the people are waiting
for the bus, drawing circles
inside the lids
of half-finished coffee cups.

black cat

I traded in my nine lives
for a One more practical
my ease and quiet
and thrill for Humdrum
outlived our adventures
from years ago
sustain and softly begin
our mold of milk and charcoal
we trade in our nine lives
for a One less eventful

stagnant

you keep moving your hands
make me a portrait
of dried leaves
put it in the garage
don't go near the back where all the
broken things are
an old humidifier and a bent chair
come here and soak in the life
of this thing that has yet to be broken

family

the strain in your throat
from making mental notes
whenever you
gulp down your food
don't forget
to breath

winter song

January
like an owl in the dark
brings new beginnings -
letters with red seals
and stockings abandoned over the fireplace
petticoats and puffers,
another long walk to school

wanda windbreaker

call me the breeze –
running along the sun
lifting light,
and smoothing corners;
call me the iridescent player –
singing sweet spring nostalgia,
notes like tufts on the trees;
sometimes, I go by windbreaker –
ruffling up the willow's hair,
and tickling her trunk 'til she shakes.

haiku dedicated to bloom (spring song)

buds sprout from meek bark
Nature's wanderer is free
her heart can now roam

purple prose

royalty in tiny
bottles of fresh ink
hues of magenta
spilt in diaries
like drink; velvet words fill pages
cover to finish
a cushion for my
ramble, my majestic cynic
lilac flamenco bound by
melancholic stitches

these hues of magenta
are the only hues I know

I leave these wounds of
plumish grape for when
I'm gone and my soul
sings through amethyst starlight
in that indigo
night; go spin my threads of
magenta – the
fruit of my life

on being perceived

my vanity
is a loose thread
trembling above a sea of
narcissi
in funhouse mirrors
I walk the tightrope
An apple in my mouth and
a hula hoop
around my waist
one day like a trapeze star
I'll soar
and abandon the spectators
trade in their cheers for cosmic love